The Fo :es

Contemplations on Love, Compassion,
Sympathetic Joy, and Equanimity

by

Nyanaponika Thera

···························· and ····························

The Practice of Loving-Kindness (*Mettā*)

As Taught by
the Buddha in the Pali Canon

Texts compiled and translated by

Ñāṇamoli Thera

BPE

BPS PARIYATTI EDITIONS

BPS Pariyatti Editions
an imprint of
Pariyatti Publishing
www.pariyatti.org

Published by Buddhist Publication Society, Kandy, Sri Lanka.

The Four Sublime States: 1958, 1960, 1972, 1980,1993, 2006, 2013.
The Practice of Loving Kindness: 1958, 1964, 1978, 1981, 1987, 2006, 2013.

Published with the consent of the original publisher.

First BPS Pariyatti Edition, 2021
ISBN: 978-1-68172-385-3 (Print)
ISBN: 978-1-68172-388-4 (PDF)
ISBN: 978-1-68172-386-0 (ePub)
ISBN: 978-1-68172-387-7 (Mobi)
LCCN: 2021936602

CONTENTS

The Four Sublime States

The Practice of Loving-Kindness (*Mettā*)

The Four Sublime States

Contemplations on Love, Compassion, Sympathetic Joy, and Equanimity

by

Nyanaponika Thera

INTRODUCTION

Four sublime states of mind have been taught by the Buddha:

> Love, or loving-kindness (*mettā*),
> Compassion (*karuṇā*),
> Sympathetic Joy (*muditā*),
> Equanimity (*upekkhā*).

In Pali, the language of the Buddhist scriptures, these four are known as *Brahma-vihāra*, a term which may be rendered as excellent, lofty, or sublime states of mind; or alternatively, as Brahma-like, god-like, or divine abodes.

These four attitudes are said to be *excellent* or *sublime* because they are the right or ideal way of conduct towards living beings (*sattesu sammā paṭipatti*). They provide, in fact, the answer to all situations arising from social contact. They are the great removers of tension, the great peace-makers in social conflict, and the great healers of wounds suffered in the struggle of existence. They level social barriers, build harmonious communities, awaken slumbering magnanimity long forgotten, revive joy and hope long abandoned, and promote human brotherhood against the forces of egotism.

The Brahma-vihāras are incompatible with a hating state of mind, and in that they are akin to Brahmā, the divine but transient ruler of the higher heavens in the traditional Buddhist picture of the universe. In contrast to many other conceptions of deities, East and West, who by their own devotees are said to show anger, wrath, jealousy, and "righteous indignation," Brahmā is free from hate; and one who assiduously develops these four sublime states, by conduct and meditation, is said to become an equal of Brahmā (*brahma-samo*). If they become the dominant influence in one's mind, one will be reborn in congenial worlds, the realms of Brahmā. Therefore these states of mind are called *god-like, Brahma-like.*

They are called *abodes* (*vihāra*) because they should become the mind's constant dwelling-places where we feel "at home"; they should not remain merely places of rare and short visits, soon forgotten. In other words, our minds should become thoroughly saturated by them. They should become our inseparable companions, and we should be mindful of them in all our common activities. As the Mettā Sutta, the Song of Loving-Kindness, says:

> When standing, walking, sitting, lying down,
> Whenever one feels free of tiredness
> Let one establish well this mindfulness—
> This, it is said, is the Divine Abode.

These four—love, compassion, sympathetic joy, and equanimity—are also known as the *boundless states* (*appamaññā*), because, in their perfection and their true nature, they should not be narrowed by any limitation as to the range of beings towards whom they are extended. They should be non-exclusive and impartial, not bound by selective preferences or prejudices. A mind that has attained to that boundlessness of the Brahma-vihāras will not harbour any national, racial, religious, or class hatred.

But unless rooted in a strong natural affinity with such a mental attitude, it will certainly not be easy for us to effect that boundless application by a deliberate effort of will and to avoid consistently any kind or degree of partiality. To achieve that, in most cases, we shall have to use these four qualities not only as principles of conduct and objects of reflection but also as subjects of methodical meditation. That meditation is called *brahma-vihāra-bhāvanā*, the meditative development of the sublime states.

The practical aim is to achieve, with the help of these sublime states, those high stages of mental concentration called *jhāna*, "meditative absorption." The meditations on love, compassion, and sympathetic joy can each produce the attainment of the first three absorptions, while the meditation on equanimity will lead to the fourth only, in which equanimity is the most significant factor.

Generally speaking, persistent meditative practice will have two crowning effects: first, it will make these four qualities sink deep into the heart so that they become spontaneous attitudes not easily overthrown; and second, it will bring out and secure their *boundless* extension, the unfolding of their all-embracing range. In fact, the detailed instructions given in the Buddhist scriptures for the practice of these four meditations are clearly intended to gradually unfold the boundlessness of the sublime states. They systematically break down all barriers restricting their application to particular individuals or places.

In the meditative exercises, the selection of people to whom the thought of love, compassion, or sympathetic joy is directed, proceeds from the easier to the more difficult. For instance, when meditating on loving-kindness, one starts with an aspiration for one's own well-being, using it as a point of reference for gradual extension: "Just as I wish to be happy and free from suffering, so may *that* being ... may *all* beings be happy and free from suffering!" Then one extends the thought of loving-kindness to a person for whom one has a loving respect, as, for instance, a teacher; then to dearly beloved people, to indifferent ones, and finally to enemies, if any, or those disliked. Since this meditation is concerned with the welfare of the living, one should not choose people who have died; one should also avoid choosing people towards whom one may have feelings of sexual attraction.

After one has been able to cope with the hardest task, to direct one's thoughts of loving-kindness to disagreeable people, one should now "break down the barriers" (*sīma-sambheda*). Without making any discrimination between those four types of people, one should extend one's loving-kindness to them equally. At that point of the practice one will have come to the higher stages of concentration: with the appearance of the mental reflex-image (*paṭibhāga-nimitta*), "access concentration" (*upacāra-samādhi*) will have been reached, and further progress will lead to the full concentration (*appanā*) of the first jhāna, then the higher jhānas.

For spatial expansion, the practice starts with those in one's immediate environment such as one's family, then extends to one's neighbours, to the whole street, the town, country, other countries, and the entire world. In "pervasion of the directions," one's thought of loving-kindness is directed first to the east, then to the west, north, south, the intermediate directions, the zenith, and nadir.

The same principles of practice apply to the meditative development of compassion, sympathetic joy, and equanimity, with due variations in the selection of people. Details of the practice will be found in the texts (see *Visuddhimagga*, Chapter IX).

The ultimate aim of attaining the jhānas on the Brahma-vihāras is to produce a state of mind that can serve as a firm basis for the liberating insight into the true nature of all phenomena, as being impermanent, liable to suffering, and unsubstantial. A mind that has achieved meditative absorption induced by the sublime states will be pure, tranquil, firm, collected, and free of coarse selfishness. It will thus be well prepared for the final work of deliverance that can be completed only by insight.

The preceding remarks show that there are two ways of developing the sublime states: first by practical conduct and an appropriate direction of thought; and second by methodical meditation aiming at the absorptions. Each will prove helpful to the other. Methodical meditative practice will help love, compassion, joy, and equanimity to become spontaneous. It will help make the mind firmer and calmer in withstanding the numerous irritations in life that challenge us to maintain these four qualities in thoughts, words, and deeds.

On the other hand, if one's practical conduct is increasingly governed by these sublime states, the mind will harbour less resentment, tension, and irritability, the reverberations of which often subtly intrude into the hours of meditation, forming there the "hindrance of restlessness." Our everyday life and thought have a strong influence on the meditative mind; only if the gap between them is persistently narrowed will there be a chance for steady meditative progress and for achieving the highest aim of our practice.

Meditative development of the sublime states will be aided by repeated reflection upon their qualities, the benefits they bestow, and the dangers from their opposites. As the Buddha says, "What a person considers and reflects upon for a long time, to that his mind will bend and incline."

The Basic Passage on the
Four Sublime States

From the Discourses of the Buddha

I

Here, monks, a disciple dwells pervading one direction with his heart filled with loving-kindness, likewise the second, the third, and the fourth directions; so above, below, and around; he dwells pervading the entire world everywhere and equally with his heart filled with loving-kindness, abundant, grown great, measureless, free from enmity, and free from distress.

II

Here, monks, a disciple dwells pervading one direction with his heart filled with compassion, likewise the second, the third, and the fourth directions; so above, below, and around; he dwells pervading the entire world everywhere and equally with his heart filled with compassion, abundant, grown great, measureless, free from enmity, and free from distress.

III

Here, monks, a disciple dwells pervading one direction with his heart filled with sympathetic joy, likewise the second, the third, and the fourth directions; so above, below, and around; he dwells pervading the entire world everywhere and equally with his heart filled with sympathetic joy, abundant, grown great, measureless, free from enmity, and free from distress.

IV

Here, monks, a disciple dwells pervading one direction with his heart filled with equanimity, likewise the second, the third, and the fourth directions; so above, below, and around; he dwells pervading the entire world everywhere and equally with his heart filled with equanimity, abundant, grown great, measureless, free from enmity, and free from distress.

Dīgha Nikāya 13

Contemplations on the Four Sublime States

I

Love (*Mettā*)

Love, without desire to possess, knowing well that in the ultimate sense there is no possession and no possessor: this is the highest love.

Love, without speaking and thinking of "I," knowing well that this so-called "I" is a mere delusion.

Love, without selecting and excluding, knowing well that to do so means to create love's own contrasts: dislike, aversion, and hatred.

Love, embracing all beings: small and great, far and near, be it on earth, in the water, or in the air.

Love, embracing impartially all sentient beings, and not only those who are useful, pleasing, or amusing to us.

Love, embracing all beings, be they noble-minded or low-minded, good or evil. The noble and the good are embraced because love is flowing to them spontaneously. The low-minded and evil-minded are included because they are those who are most in need of love. In many of them the seed of goodness may have died merely because warmth was lacking for its growth, because it perished from cold in a loveless world.

Love, embracing all beings, knowing well that we all are fellow wayfarers through this round of existence—that we all are overcome by the same law of suffering.

Love, but not the sensuous fire that burns, scorches and tortures, that inflicts more wounds than it cures—flaring up now, at the next moment being extinguished, leaving behind more coldness and loneliness than was felt before.

Rather, love that lies like a soft but firm hand on the ailing beings, ever unchanged in its sympathy, without wavering, unconcerned with any response it meets. Love that is comforting coolness to those who burn with the fire of suffering and passion; that is life-giving warmth to those abandoned in the cold desert of loneliness, to those who are shivering in the frost of a loveless world; to those whose hearts have become as if empty and dry by the repeated calls for help, by deepest despair.

Love, that is a sublime nobility of heart and intellect which knows, understands, and is ready to help.

Love, that is strength and gives strength: this is the highest love.

Love, which by the Enlightened One was named "the liberation of the heart," "the most sublime beauty": this is the highest love.

And what is the highest manifestation of love?

To show to the world the path leading to the end of suffering, the path pointed out, trodden, and realized to perfection by Him, the Exalted One, the Buddha.

II

Compassion (*Karuṇā*)

The world suffers. But most people have their eyes and ears closed. They do not see the unbroken stream of tears flowing through life; they do not hear the cry of distress continually pervading the world. Their own little grief or joy bars their sight, deafens their ears. Bound by selfishness, their hearts turn stiff and narrow. Being stiff and narrow, how should they be able to strive for any higher goal, to realize that only release from selfish craving will effect their own freedom from suffering?

It is compassion that removes the heavy bar, opens the door to freedom, makes the narrow heart as wide as the world. Compassion takes away from the heart the inert weight, the paralyzing heaviness; it gives wings to those who cling to the lowlands of self.

Through compassion the fact of suffering remains vividly present to our mind, even at times when we personally are free from it. It gives us the rich experience of suffering, thus strengthening us to meet it prepared when it does befall us.

Compassion reconciles us to our own destiny by showing us the lives of others, often much harder than ours.

Behold the endless caravan of beings, men and beasts, burdened with sorrow and pain! The burden of every one of them, we also have carried in bygone times during the unfathomable sequence of repeated births. Behold this, and open your heart to compassion!

And this misery may well be our own destiny again! One who is without compassion now will one day cry for it. If sympathy with others is lacking, it will have to be acquired through one's own long and painful experience. This is the great law of life. Knowing this, keep guard over yourself!

Beings, sunk in ignorance, lost in delusion, hasten from one state of suffering to another, not knowing the real cause, not knowing the escape from it. This insight into the general law of suffering is the real foundation of our compassion, not any isolated fact of suffering.

Hence our compassion will also include those who at the moment may be happy, but act with an evil and deluded mind. In their present deeds we shall foresee their future state of distress, and compassion will arise.

The compassion of the wise man does not render him a victim of suffering. His thoughts, words, and deeds are full of pity. But his heart does not waver; unchanged it remains, serene and calm. How else should he be able to help?

May such compassion arise in our hearts! Compassion that is sublime nobility of heart and intellect which knows, understands, and is ready to help.

Compassion that is strength and gives strength: this is highest compassion.

And what is the highest manifestation of compassion?

To show to the world the path leading to the end of suffering, the path pointed out, trodden, and realized to perfection by Him, the Exalted One, the Buddha.

III

Sympathetic Joy (*Muditā*)

Not only to compassion, but also to joy with others open your heart!

Small, indeed, is the share of happiness and joy allotted to beings! Whenever a little happiness comes to them, then you may rejoice that at least one ray of joy has pierced through the darkness of their lives, and dispelled the gray and gloomy mist that enwraps their hearts.

Your life will gain in joy by sharing the happiness of others as if it were yours. Did you never observe how in moments of happiness people's features change and become bright with joy? Did you never notice how joy rouses people to noble aspirations and deeds, exceeding their normal capacity? Did not such experience fill your own heart with joyful bliss? It is in your power to increase such experience of sympathetic joy, by producing happiness in others, by bringing them joy and solace.

Let us teach real joy to people! Many have unlearned it. Life, though full of woe, holds also sources of happiness and joy, unknown to most. Let us teach people to seek and to find real joy within themselves and to rejoice with the joy of others! Let us teach them to unfold their joy to ever sublimer heights! Noble and sublime joy is not foreign to the Teaching of the Enlightened One. Wrongly the Buddha's Teaching is sometimes considered to be a doctrine diffusing melancholy. Far from it: the Dhamma leads step by step to an ever purer and loftier happiness.

Noble and sublime joy is a helper on the path to the extinction of suffering. Not one who is depressed by grief, but one possessed of joy finds that serene calmness leading to a contemplative state of mind. And only a mind serene and collected is able to gain the liberating wisdom.

The more sublime and noble the joy of others is, the more justified will be our own sympathetic joy. A cause for our joy with others is their noble life securing them happiness here and in lives hereafter. A still nobler cause for our joy with others is their faith in the Dhamma, their understanding of the Dhamma, their following the Dhamma. Let us give them the help of the Dhamma! Let us strive to become more and more able ourselves to render such help!

Sympathetic joy means a sublime nobility of heart and intellect which knows, understands, and is ready to help.

Sympathetic joy that is strength and gives strength: this is the highest joy.

And what is the highest manifestation of sympathetic joy?

To show to the world the path leading to the end of suffering, the path pointed out, trodden, and realized to perfection by Him, the Exalted One, the Buddha.

IV

Equanimity (*Upekkhā*)

Equanimity is a perfect, unshakable balance of mind, rooted in insight.

Looking at the world around us, and looking into our own heart, we see clearly how difficult it is to attain and maintain balance of mind.

Looking into life we notice how it continually moves between contrasts: rise and fall, success and failure, loss and gain, honour and blame. We feel how our heart responds to all this with happiness and sorrow, delight and despair, disappointment and satisfaction, hope and fear. These waves of emotion carry us up and fling us down; and no sooner do we find rest, than we are in the power of a new wave again. How can we expect to get a footing on the crest of the waves? How can we erect the building of our lives in the midst of this ever restless ocean of existence, if not on the Island of Equanimity.

A world where that little share of happiness allotted to beings is mostly secured after many disappointments, failures, and defeats;

a world where only the courage to start anew, again and again, promises success;

a world where scanty joy grows amidst sickness, separation, and death;

a world where beings who were a short while ago connected to us by sympathetic joy, are at the next moment in want of our compassion—such a world needs equanimity.

But the kind of equanimity required has to be based on vigilant presence of mind, not on indifferent dullness. It has to be the result of hard, deliberate training, not the casual outcome of a passing mood. But equanimity would not deserve its name if it had to be produced by exertion again and again. In such a case it would surely be weakened and finally defeated by the vicissitudes of life. True equanimity, however, should be able to meet all these severe tests and to regenerate its strength from sources within. It will possess this power of resistance and self-renewal only if it is rooted in insight.

What, now, is the nature of that insight? It is the clear understanding of how all these vicissitudes of life originate, and of our own true nature. We have to understand that the various experiences we undergo result from our *kamma*—our actions in thought, word, and deed—performed in this life and in earlier lives. Kamma is the womb from which we spring (*kamma-yoni*), and whether we like it or not, we are the inalienable "owners" of our deeds (*kammassaka*). But as soon as we have performed any action, our control over it is lost: it forever remains with us and inevitably returns to us as our due heritage (*kamma-dāyāda*). Nothing that happens to us comes from an "outer" hostile world foreign to ourselves; everything is the outcome of our own mind and deeds. Because this knowledge frees us from fear, it is the first basis of equanimity. When, in everything that befalls us we only meet ourselves, why should we fear?

If, however, fear or uncertainty should arise, we know the refuge where it can be allayed: our good deeds (*kamma-paṭisaraṇa*). By taking this refuge, confidence and courage will grow within us—confidence in the protecting power of our good deeds done in the past; courage to perform more good deeds right now, despite the discouraging hardships of our present life. For we know that noble and selfless deeds provide the best defence against the hard blows of destiny, that it is never too late but always the right time for good actions. If that refuge, in doing good and avoiding evil, becomes firmly established within us, one day we shall feel assured: "More and more ceases the misery and evil rooted in the past. And this present life—I try to make it spotless and pure. What else can the future bring than increase of the good?" And from that certainty our minds will become serene, and we shall gain the strength of patience and equanimity to bear with all our present adversities. Then our deeds will be our friends (*kamma-bandhu*).

Likewise, all the various events of our lives, being the result of our deeds, will also be our friends, even if they bring us sorrow and pain. Our deeds return to us in a guise that often makes them unrecognizable. Sometimes our actions return to us in the way that others treat us, sometimes as a thorough upheaval in our lives; often the results are against our expectations or contrary to our wills. Such experiences point out to us consequences of our deeds we did not foresee; they render visible half-conscious motives of our former actions which we tried to hide even from ourselves, covering them up with various pretexts. If we learn to see things from this angle, and to read the message conveyed by our own experience, then suffering, too, will be our friend. It will be a stern friend, but a truthful and well-meaning one who teaches us the most difficult subject, knowledge about ourselves, and warns us against abysses towards which we are moving blindly. By looking at suffering as our teacher and friend, we shall better succeed in enduring it with equanimity. Consequently, the teaching of kamma will give us a powerful impulse for freeing ourselves from kamma, from those deeds which again and again throw us into the suffering of repeated births. Disgust will arise at our own craving, at our own delusion, at our own propensity to create situations which try our strength, our resistance, and our equanimity.

The second insight on which equanimity should be based is the Buddha's teaching of non-self (*anattā*). This doctrine shows that in the ultimate sense deeds are not performed by any self, nor do their results affect any self. Further, it shows that if there is no self, we cannot speak of "my own." It is the delusion of a self that creates suffering and hinders or disturbs equanimity. If this or that quality of ours is blamed, one thinks: "I am blamed" and equanimity is shaken. If this or that work does not succeed, one thinks: "My work has failed" and equanimity is shaken. If wealth or loved ones are lost, one thinks: "What is mine has gone" and equanimity is shaken.

To establish equanimity as an unshakable state of mind, one has to give up all possessive thoughts of "mine," beginning with little things from which it is easy to detach oneself, and gradually working up to possessions and aims to which one's whole heart clings. One also has to give up the counterpart to such thoughts, all egoistic thoughts of "self," beginning with a small section of one's personality, with qualities of minor importance, with small weaknesses one clearly sees, and gradually working up to those emotions and aversions which one regards as the centre of one's being. Thus detachment should be practised.

To the degree we forsake thoughts of "mine" or "self," equanimity will enter our hearts. For how can anything we realize to be foreign and void of a self cause us agitation due to lust, hatred, or grief? Thus the teaching of non-self will be our guide on the path to deliverance, to perfect equanimity.

Equanimity is the crown and culmination of the four sublime states. But this should not be understood to mean that equanimity is the negation of love, compassion, and sympathetic joy, or that it leaves them behind as inferior. Far from that, equanimity includes and pervades them fully, just as they fully pervade perfect equanimity.

The Interrelations of the Four Sublime States

How, then, do these four sublime states pervade and suffuse each other?

Unbounded love guards compassion against turning into partiality, prevents it from making discriminations by selecting and excluding, and thus protects it from falling into partiality or aversion against the excluded side.

Love imparts to equanimity its selflessness, its boundless nature, and even its fervour. For fervour, too, transformed and controlled, is part of perfect equanimity, strengthening its power of keen penetration and wise restraint.

Compassion prevents love and sympathetic joy from forgetting that, while both are enjoying or giving temporary and limited happiness, there still exist at that time most dreadful states of suffering in the world. It reminds them that their happiness coexists with measureless misery, perhaps at the next doorstep. It is a reminder to love and sympathetic joy that there is more suffering in the world than they are able to mitigate; that, after the effect of such mitigation has vanished, sorrow and pain are sure to arise anew until suffering is uprooted entirely at the attainment of Nibbāna. Compassion does not allow love and sympathetic joy to shut themselves up against the wide world by confining themselves to a narrow sector of it. Compassion prevents love and sympathetic joy from turning into states of self-satisfied complacency within a jealously-guarded petty happiness. Compassion stirs and urges love to widen its sphere; it stirs and urges sympathetic joy to search for fresh nourishment. Thus it helps both of them to grow into truly boundless states (*appamaññā*).

Compassion guards equanimity from falling into a cold indifference, and keeps it from indolent or selfish isolation. Until equanimity has reached perfection, compassion urges it to enter again and again the battle of the world, in order to be able to stand the test, by hardening and strengthening itself.

Sympathetic joy holds compassion back from becoming overwhelmed by the sight of the world's suffering, from being absorbed by it to the exclusion of everything else. Sympathetic joy relieves the tension of mind, soothes the painful burning of the compassionate heart. It keeps compassion away from melancholic brooding without purpose, from a futile sentimentality that merely weakens and consumes the strength of mind and heart. Sympathetic joy develops compassion into active sympathy.

Sympathetic joy gives to equanimity the mild serenity that softens its stern appearance. It is the divine smile on the face of the Enlightened One, a smile that persists in spite of his deep knowledge of the world's suffering, a smile that gives solace and hope, fearlessness and confidence: "Wide open are the doors to deliverance," thus it speaks.

Equanimity rooted in insight is the guiding and restraining power for the other three sublime states. It points out to them the direction they have to take, and sees to it that this direction is followed. Equanimity guards love and compassion from being dissipated in vain quests and from going astray in the labyrinths of uncontrolled emotion. Equanimity, being a vigilant self-control for the sake of the final goal, does not allow sympathetic joy to rest content with humble results, forgetting the real aims we have to strive for.

Equanimity, which means "even-mindedness," gives to love an even, unchanging firmness and loyalty. It endows it with the great virtue of patience. Equanimity furnishes compassion with an even, unwavering courage and fearlessness, enabling it to face the awesome abyss of misery and despair which confront boundless compassion again and again. To the active side of compassion, equanimity is the calm and firm hand led by wisdom—indispensable to those who want to practice the difficult art of helping others. And here again equanimity means patience, the patient devotion to the work of compassion.

In these and other ways equanimity may be said to be the crown and culmination of the other three sublime states. The first three, if unconnected with equanimity and insight, may dwindle away due to the lack of a stabilizing factor. Isolated virtues, if unsupported by other qualities which give them either the needed firmness or pliancy, often deteriorate into their own characteristic defects. For instance, loving-kindness, without energy and insight, may easily degenerate into a mere sentimental goodness of weak and unreliable nature. Moreover, such isolated virtues may often carry us in a direction contrary to our original aims and contrary to the welfare of others, too. It is the firm and balanced character of a person that knits isolated virtues into an organic and harmonious whole, within which the single qualities exhibit their best manifestations and avoid the pitfalls of their respective weaknesses. And this is the very function of equanimity, the way it contributes to an ideal relationship between all four sublime states.

Equanimity is a perfect, unshakable balance of mind, rooted in insight. But in its perfection and unshakable nature equanimity is not dull, heartless, and frigid. Its perfection is not due to an emotional "emptiness," but to a "fullness" of understanding, to its being complete in itself. Its unshakable nature is not the immovability of a dead, cold stone, but the manifestation of the highest strength.

In what way, now, is equanimity perfect and unshakable?

Whatever causes stagnation is here destroyed, what dams up is removed, what obstructs is destroyed. Vanished are the whirls of emotion and the meanderings of intellect. Unhindered goes the calm and majestic stream of consciousness, pure and radiant. Watchful mindfulness (*sati*) has harmonized the warmth of faith (*saddhā*) with the penetrative keenness of wisdom (*paññā*); it has balanced strength of will (*viriya*) with calmness of mind (*samādhi*); and these five inner faculties (*indriya*) have grown into inner forces (*bala*) that cannot be lost again. They cannot be lost because they do not lose themselves any more in the labyrinths of the world (*saṃsāra*), in the endless diffuseness of life (*papañca*). These inner forces emanate from the mind and act upon the world, but being guarded by mindfulness, they nowhere bind themselves, and they return unchanged. Love, compassion and sympathetic joy continue to emanate from the mind and act upon the world, but being guarded by equanimity, they cling nowhere, and return unweakened and unsullied.

Thus within the *Arahat*, the Liberated One, nothing is lessened by giving, and he does not become poorer by bestowing upon others the riches of his heart and mind. The Arahat is like the clear, well-cut crystal which, being without stains, fully absorbs all the rays of light and sends them out again, intensified by its concentrative power. The rays cannot stain the crystal with their various colours. They cannot pierce its hardness, nor disturb its harmonious structure. In its genuine purity and strength, the crystal remains unchanged. "Just as all the streams of the world enter the great ocean, and all the waters of the sky rain into it, but no increase or decrease of the great ocean is to be seen"—even so is the nature of holy equanimity.

Holy equanimity, or—as we may likewise express it—the Arahat endowed with holy equanimity, is the inner centre of the world. But this inner centre should be well distinguished from the numberless apparent centres of limited spheres; that is, their so-called "personalities," governing laws, and so on. All of these are only apparent centres, because they cease to be centres whenever their spheres, obeying the laws of impermanence, undergo a total change of their structure; and consequently the centre of their gravity, material or mental, will shift. But the inner centre of the Arahat's equanimity is unshakable, because it is immutable. It is immutable because it clings to nothing.

Says the Master:

"For one who clings, motion exists; but for one who clings not, there is no motion. Where no motion is, there is stillness. Where stillness is, there is no craving. Where no craving is, there is neither coming nor going. Where no coming nor going is, there is neither arising nor passing away. Where neither arising nor passing away is, there is neither this world nor a world beyond, nor a state between. This, indeed, is the end of suffering."

Udāna 8.4

The Practice of Loving-Kindness (*Mettā*)

As Taught by the Buddha in the Pali Canon

Texts compiled and translated by

Ñāṇamoli Thera

INTRODUCTION

The word "love"—one of the most compelling in the English language—is commonly used for purposes so widely separated, so gross and so rarefied, as to render it sometimes nearly meaningless. Yet rightly understood, love is the indispensable and essential foundation no less for the growth and purification of the individual as for the construction of a peaceful, progressive, and healthy society.

Now love can be considered in two principal moods: that of lovers for each other, and that of a mother for her child. In its spiritualized form, love can draw its inspiration from either the one or the other. Spiritual love idealizing the love of lovers is often conceived as a consuming flame, and then it sometimes aspires to purification through torture and the violence of martyrdom. But spiritual love that looks for guidance to the love of a mother for her child uplifts itself to the ideal of the pure fount of all safety, welfare, and spiritual health (and a mother best serves her child if she guards her own health). It is this latter kind which the Buddha takes as the basis for his teaching of universal love.

Where Greek distinguishes between sensual *eros* and spiritual *agape*, English makes do with only the one word "love." But Pali, like Sanskrit, has many words covering many shades of meaning. The word chosen by the Buddha for this teaching is *mettā*, from *mitta*, a friend (or better "the true friend in need").

Mettā in the Buddha's teaching finds its place as the first of four kinds of contemplation designed to develop a sound pacific relationship to other living beings. The four are: *mettā*, which will be rendered here by "loving-kindness," *karuṇā*, which is "compassion" or "pity," *mudita*, which is "gladness at others' success," and *upekkha*, which is "onlooking equanimity." These four are called "divine abodes" (*brahma-vihāra*), perhaps because whoever can maintain any one of them in being for even a moment has lived for that moment as do the *brahma-deva*, the highest gods.

In the Buddha's teaching these four divine abidings, the "greatest of all worldly merit," if practised alone, without insight into the true nature of existence, can lead to rebirth in the highest heavens. But all heavenly existence is without exception impermanent, and at the end of the heavenly lifespan—no matter how long it may last—the being dies and is reborn according to his or her past actions. This is because some craving for existence (for being or even for non-being), and some sort of view of existence that is not in conformity with truth, still remain latent in that person, to burst out again when the result of the good actions is spent. And where one will be reborn after that is unpredictable though it is certain that one will be reborn.

The Buddha's teaching of insight is—in as few words as possible—the training in knowledge and seeing of how it is that anything, whatever it may be whether objective or subjective, comes to be; how it acquires existence only in dependence on conditions, and is impermanent because none of the conditions for its existence is permanent; and how existence, always complex and impermanent, is never safe from pain, and is in need of a self—the will-o'-the-wisp idea, the rainbow mirage, which lures it on, and which it can never find; for the comforting illusion has constantly to be renewed. And that teaching also shows how there is a true way out from fear of pain. In its concise form this is expressed as the Four Noble Truths: the truth of suffering, the truth of suffering's origin (craving or need), the truth of suffering's cessation (through abandonment of craving), and the truth of the way leading to suffering's cessation. These four truths are called the teaching peculiar to Buddhas (*buddhānaṃ sāmukkaṃsika-desanā*) since the discovery of them is what distinguishes Buddhas.

The way (the fourth truth) is also called the Middle Way because it avoids the two extremes of sensual indulgence and of self-mortification. Its eight members are: right view, right intention, right speech, right action, right livelihood, right effort, right mindfulness, and right concentration. The practice of loving-kindness alone will give effect in some measure to all the members except the first: but it is only with right view (without self-deception) that Nibbana can be reached. Right view gives insight into the real nature of existence of being and non-being, with all its mirages and deceptions, and it is only with its help that the practice of loving-kindness is perfected, lifted out of the impermanence of even the highest heavens, and directed to the true cessation of suffering.

That true cessation comes with the elimination of deception by wrong views and with the exhaustion of the stream of craving in its two forms of lust and hate. This extinction of lust, hate, and delusion, is called Nibbāna.

✻ ✻ ✻

The discourses that follow show (in that order) the wretchedness of all anger and hate (there is no righteous anger in the Buddha's teaching); the rewards of loving-kindness; the practice of loving-kindness as a meditation and contemplation; its result in rebirth; the seeing of all things and all existence as impermanent, suffering, and non-self that is needed in order to have a vision in conformity with truth, without which the first stage of unshakable deliverance cannot be reached (for it is with this insight into how being comes to be that it is seen why the price of birth and life, even in heaven, is death); and lastly the attainment of Arahatship, by which all lust, hate, and delusion is overcome, lust for being and even for non-being cured, and rebirth ended for good.

But first, before coming to these discourses, some details from the meditation manual, the *Visuddhimagga* or "Path of Purification," will not be out of place.

Mettā (loving-kindness) is defined as follows: "Loving-kindness has the mode of friendliness for its characteristic. Its natural function is to promote friendliness. It is manifested as the disappearance of ill-will. Its footing is seeing with kindness. When it succeeds it eliminates ill-will. When it fails it degenerates into selfish affectionate desire."

The *Visuddhimagga* recommends going to some quiet place, where one can sit down in a comfortable position. Then, before starting the actual meditation, it is helpful to consider the dangers in hate and the benefits offered by forbearance: for it is a purpose of this meditation to displace hate by forbearance, and besides, one cannot avoid dangers one has not come to see or cultivate benefits one does not yet know.

Then there are certain types of persons towards whom loving-kindness should not be developed in the first stages. The attempt, at the outset to regard a disliked person as dear to one is fatiguing, and likewise trying to regard a dearly loved friend with neutrality, and when an enemy is recalled anger springs up. Again, it should not be directed towards members of the opposite sex to begin with, for this may arouse lust. Right at the start, the meditation of loving-kindness should be developed towards oneself repeatedly in this way: "May I be happy and free from suffering," or "May I keep myself free from hostility and trouble and live happily" (though this will never produce the full absorption of contemplation). It is by cultivating the thought "May I be happy" with oneself as example, that one begins to be interested in the welfare and happiness of other living beings, and to feel in some sense their happiness as if it were one's own: "Just as I want happiness and fear pain, just as I want to live and not to die, so do other beings." So one should first become familiar with pervading oneself as an example with loving-kindness. Only then should one choose someone who is liked and admired and much respected. The meditation can then be developed towards that person, remembering endearing words or virtues of his, and thinking such thoughts about him as "May he be happy." (In this way the full absorption of contemplation, in which the word-meditation is left behind, can be attained.)

When this has become familiar, one can begin to practise loving-kindness towards a dearly beloved companion, and then towards a neutral person as very dear, or towards an enemy as neutral. It is when dealing with an enemy that anger can arise, and all means must be tried in order to get rid of it. As soon as this has succeeded, one will be able to regard an enemy without resentment and with loving-kindness in the same way as one does the admired person, the dearly loved friend, and the neutral person. Then with repeated practice, jhāna absorption should be attained in all cases. Loving-kindness can now be effectively maintained in being towards all beings; or to certain groups of beings at a time, or in one direction at a time to all; or to certain groups in succession.

Loving-kindness ought to be brought to the point where there are no longer any barriers set between persons, and for this the following example is given: Suppose a man is with a dear, a neutral, and a hostile person, himself being the fourth; then bandits come to him and say, "We need one of you for human sacrifice." Now, if that man thinks, "Let them take this one, or that one," he has not yet broken down the barriers; and also if he thinks, "Let them take me but not these three," he has not broken down the barriers either. Why not? Because he seeks the harm of the one whom he wishes to be taken and the welfare of only the other three. It is only when he does not see a single one among the four to be chosen in preference to the other three, and directs his mind quite impartially towards himself and the other three, that he has broken down the barriers.

Loving-kindness has its "enemy within" in lust, which easily gains entry in its wake, and it must be well guarded against this. The remedy for lust is the contemplation of foulness (in the body) as in the Satipaṭṭhāna Sutta (Dīgha Nikāya Sutta No. 22 and Majjhima Nikāya Sutta No. 10). Its "enemy without" is its opposite, ill-will, which finds its opportunities in the intervals when loving-kindness is not being actively practised. (Full details will be found in Chapter IX of the *Visuddhimagga*.)

In many discourses the Buddha lays emphasis on the need to balance contemplative concentration with understanding. The one supplies the deficiencies of the other. Concentration alone lacks direction; understanding alone is dry and tiring. In the discourses that follow the simile of a mother's love for her child is given. Now the incomparable value of a mother's love, which sets it above all other kinds, lies in the fact that she understands her child's welfare—her love is not blind. Not love alone, nor faith alone, can ever bring one all the way to the cessation of suffering, and that is why the Buddha, as the Supreme Physician, prescribes the development of five faculties in balanced harmony: the faculties of faith, energy, mindfulness, concentration, and understanding.

So concentration of love in its highest form—the form that only the Buddha, and no one else, has given—seen as a means to the end, becomes absolutely purified in one who has gained personal experience of the "supreme safety from bondage" (*anuttara yogakkhema*), which is Nibbāna, as the ultimate welfare of beings. For he knows from his own experience that their welfare is only assured permanently when suffering has been diagnosed, its origin abandoned, its cessation realized, and the way maintained in being. Then he has verified the Four Noble Truths for himself and can properly evaluate beings' welfare.

"Bhikkhus, it is through not discovering, not penetrating to four truths that both you and I have been trudging and travelling through the round of rebirths for so long" (Dīgha Nikāya II 90). For the benefit of all those who have not yet done this, the way has been discovered and pointed out by the Buddha and its practicability attested by the Arahats.

The last discourse given in this collection, in fact, shows how this personal discovery and penetration to the Four Noble Truths can be achieved by using loving-kindness as the vehicle.

Note on Sources

References to the Aṅguttara Nikāya are to *nipāta* followed by the number of the sutta. The reference to Saṃyutta Nikāya is to the *saṃyutta* followed by the number of the sutta.

The Practice of Loving-Kindness

The Wretchedness of Anger

1. *From the Aṅguttara Nikāya, 7:60*
   (spoken by the Buddha)

Bhikkhus, seven things gratifying and helpful to an enemy befall one who is angry, whether a woman or a man. What are the seven?

Here, bhikkhus, an enemy wishes thus for his enemy: "Let him be ugly." Why is that? No enemy relishes an enemy's beauty. Now when this person is angry, a prey to anger, ruled by anger, be he ever so well bathed and well anointed, with hair and beard trimmed, and clothed in white, yet he is ugly through his being a prey to anger. This is the first thing gratifying and helpful to an enemy that befalls one who is angry, whether a woman or a man.

Also an enemy wishes thus for his enemy: "Let him lie in pain." Why is that? No enemy relishes an enemy's lying in comfort. Now when this person is angry, a prey to anger, ruled by anger, for all he may lie on a couch spread with rugs, blankets, and counterpanes with a deerskin cover, a canopy, and red cushions for the head and feet, yet he lies only in pain through his being a prey to anger. This is the second thing gratifying to an enemy that befalls one who is angry, whether a woman or a man.

Also an enemy wishes thus for his enemy: "Let him have no prosperity." Why is that? No enemy relishes an enemy's prosperity. Now when this person is angry, a prey to anger, ruled by anger, he mistakes bad for good and he mistakes good for bad, and each being taken wrongly in the other's sense, these things for long conduce to his harm and suffering, through his being a prey to anger.

This is the third thing gratifying and helpful to an enemy that befalls one who is angry, whether a woman or a man.

Also an enemy wishes thus for his enemy: "Let him not be rich." Why is that? No enemy relishes an enemy's having riches. Now when a person is angry, a prey to anger, should he have riches gained by endeavour, built up by the strength of his arm, earned by sweat, lawful and lawfully acquired, yet the king's treasury gathers (in fines) through his being a prey to anger. This is the fourth thing gratifying and helpful to an enemy that befalls one who is a prey to anger, whether a woman or a man.

Also an enemy wishes thus for his enemy: "Let him not be famous." Why is that? No enemy relishes an enemy's having fame. Now when a person is angry, a prey to anger, ruled by anger, what fame he may have acquired by diligence he loses through his being a prey to anger. This is the fifth thing gratifying and helpful to an enemy that befalls one who is a prey to anger, whether a woman or a man.

Also an enemy wishes thus for his enemy: "Let him have no friends." Why is that? No enemy relishes an enemy's having friends. Now when this person is angry, a prey to anger, ruled by anger, the friends he may have, his companions, relatives, and kin, will keep away from him through his being a prey to anger. This is the sixth thing gratifying and helpful to an enemy that befalls one who is a prey to anger, whether a woman or a man.

Also an enemy wishes thus for his enemy: "Let him, on the dissolution of the body, after death, reappear in a state of deprivation, in a bad destination, in perdition, even in hell." Why is that? No enemy relishes an enemy's going to a good destination. Now when this person is angry, a prey to anger, ruled by anger, he misconducts himself in body, speech, and mind, and by his misconduct in body, speech, and mind, on the dissolution of the body, after death, he reappears in a state of deprivation, in a bad destination, in perdition, even in hell, through his being a prey to anger. This is the seventh thing gratifying and helpful to an enemy that befalls one who is angry, whether a woman or a man.

> When anger does possess a man,
> He looks ugly; he lies in pain;
> What benefit he may come by
> He misconstrues as a mischance;
> He loses property (through fines)
> Because he has been working harm
> Through acts of body and speech
> By angry passion overwhelmed;
> The wrath and rage that madden him
> Gain him a name of ill-repute;
> His fellows, relatives and kin,
> Will seek to shun him from afar;
> And anger fathers misery:
> This fury does so cloud the mind
> Of man that he cannot discern
> This fearful inner danger.
>
> An angry man no meaning knows,
> No angry man sees the Dhamma,
> So wrapped in darkness, as if blind,
> Is he whom anger dogs.
>
> Someone a man in anger hurts;
> But, when his anger is later spent
> With difficulty or with ease,
> He suffers as if seared by fire.
> His look betrays the sulkiness
> Of some dim smoky smoldering glow.

Whence may flare up an anger-blaze
That sets the world of men aflame.
He has no shame or conscience curb,
No kindly words come forth from him,
There is no island refuge for
The man whom anger dogs.

Such acts as will ensure remorse,
Such as are far from the true Dhamma:
It is of these that I would tell,
So harken to my words.

Anger makes man a parricide,
Anger makes him a matricide,
Anger can make him slay the saint
As he would kill the common man.

Nursed and reared by a mother's care,
He comes to look upon the world,
Yet the common man in anger kills
The being who gave him life.

No being but seeks his own self's good,
None dearer to him than himself,
Yet men in anger kill themselves,
Distraught for reasons manifold:
For crazed they stab themselves with daggers,
In desperation swallow poison,
Perish hanged by ropes, or fling
Themselves over a precipice.

Yet how their life-destroying acts
Bring death unto themselves as well,
That they cannot discern, and that
Is the ruin anger breeds.

This secret place, with anger's aid,
Is where mortality sets the snare.
To blot it out with discipline,
With vision, strength, and understanding,
To blot each fault out one by one,
The wise man should apply himself,
Training likewise in the true Dhamma;
"Let smoldering be far from us."

Then rid of wrath and free from anger,
And rid of lust and free from envy,
Tamed, and with anger left behind,
Taintless, they reach Nibbāna.

How to Get Rid of Anger

2. *From the Dhammapada, vv. 3–5, and Majjhima
    Nikāya, Sutta 128 (spoken by the Buddha)*

"He abused me, he beat me,
He worsted me, he robbed me."
Hate never is allayed in those
Who cherish suchlike enmity.

"He abused me, he beat me,
He worsted me, he robbed me."
Hate surely is allayed in those
Who cherish no such enmity.

For enmity by enmity
Is never in this world allayed;
It is allayed by amity—
That is an ancient principle.

3. *From the Aṅguttara Nikāya, 5:161*
   (spoken by the Buddha)

Bhikkhus, there are these five ways of removing annoyance, by which annoyance can be entirely removed by a bhikkhu when it arises in him. What are the five?

Loving-kindness can be maintained in being towards a person with whom you are annoyed: this is how annoyance with him can be removed. Compassion can be maintained in being towards a person with whom you are annoyed; this too is how annoyance with him can be removed. Equanimity can be maintained in being towards a person with whom you are annoyed; this too is how annoyance with him can be removed. The forgetting and ignoring of a person with whom you are annoyed can be practised; this too is how annoyance with him can be removed. Ownership of deeds in a person with whom you are annoyed can be concentrated upon thus: "This good person is owner of his deeds, heir to his deeds, his deeds are the womb from which he is born, his deeds are his kin for whom he is responsible, his deeds are his refuge, he is heir to his deeds, be they good or bad." This too is how annoyance with him can be removed. These are the five ways of removing annoyance, by which annoyance can be entirely removed in a bhikkhu when it arises in him.

Loving-Kindness and its Rewards

4. *From the Majjhima Nikāya, Sutta 21*
   (spoken by the Buddha)

Bhikkhus, there are five modes of speech that others may use when they address you. Their speech may be timely or untimely, true or untrue, gentle or harsh, for good or harm, and may be accompanied by thoughts of loving-kindness or by inner hate.

Suppose a man came with a hoe and a basket, and he said, "I shall make this great earth to be without earth"; and he dug here and there and strewed here and there, and spat here and there, and relieved himself here and there, saying, "Be without earth, be without earth." What do you think, bhikkhus, would that man make this great earth to be without earth?—No, venerable sir. Why is that? Because this great earth is deep and measureless; it cannot possibly be made to be without earth. So the man would reap only weariness and disappointment.

Suppose a man came with lak or gamboge or indigo or carmine, and he said, "I shall draw pictures, I shall make pictures appear, on this empty space." What do you think, bhikkhus, would that man draw pictures, would he make pictures appear, on that empty space?—No, venerable sir. Why is that? Because that empty space is formless and invisible; he cannot possibly draw pictures, make pictures appear there. So the man would reap weariness and disappointment.

So too, bhikkhus, there are these five modes of speech that others may use when they address you. Their speech may be timely or untimely, true or untrue, gentle or harsh, for good or for harm, and may be accompanied by thoughts of loving-kindness or by inner hate. Now this is how you should train yourselves here: "Our minds will remain unaffected, we shall utter no bad words, we shall abide friendly and compassionate, with thoughts of loving-kindness and no inner hate. We shall abide with loving-kindness in our hearts extending to that person, and we shall dwell extending it to the entire world as our object, with our hearts abundant, exalted, measureless in loving-kindness, without hostility or ill-will." That is how you should train yourselves.

Even were bandits savagely to sever you limb from limb with a two-handled saw, he who on that account entertained hate in his heart would not be one who carried out my teaching.

Bhikkhus, you should keep this instruction on the Simile of the Saw constantly in mind.

5.   *From the Itivuttaka, Sutta 27*
      (spoken by the Buddha)

Bhikkhus, whatever kinds of worldly merit there are, all are not worth one sixteenth part of the heart-deliverance of loving-kindness; in shining and beaming and radiance the heart-deliverance of loving-kindness far excels them.

Just as whatever light there is of stars, all is not worth one sixteenth part of the moon's; in shining and beaming and radiance the moon's light far excels it; and just as in the last month of the rains, in the autumn when the heavens are clear, the sun as it climbs the heavens drives all darkness from the sky with its shining and beaming and radiance; and just as, when night is turning to dawn, the morning star is shining and beaming and radiating; so too, whatever kinds of worldly merit there are, all are not worth one sixteenth part of the heart-deliverance of loving-kindness; in shining and beaming and radiance the heart- deliverance of loving-kindness far excels them.

6.   *From the Aṅguttara Nikāya, 11:16*
      (spoken by the Buddha)

Bhikkhus, when the heart-deliverance of loving-kindness is maintained in being, made much of, used as one's vehicle, used as one's foundation, established, consolidated, and properly managed, then eleven blessings can be expected. What are the eleven?

One sleeps in comfort; one wakes in comfort; one dreams no evil dreams; one is dear to human beings; one is dear to non-human beings; the gods guard one; no fire or poison or weapon harms one; one's mind can be quickly concentrated; the expression of one's face is serene; one dies without falling into confusion; and, even if one fails to penetrate any further, one will pass on to the world of High Divinity, to the Brahma world.

7.   *From the Saṃyutta Nikāya, 20:3*
      (spoken by the Buddha)

Bhikkhus, just as clans with many women and few men are readily ruined by robbers and bandits, so too any bhikkhu who has not maintained in being and made much of the heart-deliverance of loving-kindness is readily ruined by non-human beings. And just as clans with few women and many men are not readily ruined by robbers and bandits, so too any bhikkhu who maintains in being and makes much of the heart-deliverance of loving-kindness is not readily ruined by non-human beings.

So, bhikkhus, you should train in this way: "The heart-deliverance of loving-kindness will be maintained in being and made much of by us, used as our vehicle, used as our foundation, established, consolidated, and properly managed." That is how you should train.

8.   *From the Aṅguttara Nikāya, 1:53–55, 386*
      (spoken by the Buddha)

Bhikkhus, if a bhikkhu cultivates loving-kindness for as long as a fingersnap, he is called a bhikkhu. He is not destitute of *jhāna* meditation, he carries out the Master's teaching, he responds to advice, and he does not eat the country's almsfood in vain. So what should be said of those who make much of it?

9. *From the Dīgha Nikāya, Sutta 33*
   (spoken by the Arahat Sāriputta)

Here, friends, a bhikkhu might say: "When the heart-deliverance of loving-kindness is maintained in being and made much of by me, used as my vehicle, used as my foundation, established, consolidated, and properly managed, ill-will nevertheless still invades my heart and remains." He should be told: "Not so! Let the worthy one not say so. Let him not misrepresent the Blessed One. It is not good to misrepresent the Blessed One. The Blessed One would not express it thus." Friends, it is impossible, it cannot happen, that when the heart-deliverance of loving-kindness is maintained in being and made much of, used as one's vehicle, used as one's foundation, established, consolidated, and properly managed, ill-will can invade the heart and remain; for this, that is to say, the heart-deliverance of loving-kindness, is the escape from ill-will.

Loving-Kindness as a Contemplation

10. *Mettā Sutta From the Sutta-nipāta, vv. 143–152*
    (spoken by the Buddha)

What should be done by one skillful in good
So as to gain the State of Peace is this:

Let him be able, and upright and straight,
Easy to speak to, gentle, and not proud,
Contented too, supported easily,
With few tasks, and living very lightly;
His faculties serene, prudent, and modest,
Unswayed by the emotions of the clans;
And let him never do the slightest thing
That other wise men might hold blameable.

(And let him think:) "In safety and in bliss
May creatures all be of a blissful heart!
Whatever breathing beings there may be,
No matter whether they are frail or firm,
With none excepted, be they long or big
Or middle-sized, or be they short or small
Or thick, as well as those seen or unseen,
Or whether they are dwelling far or near,
Existing or yet seeking to exist.
May creatures all be of a blissful heart!

Let no one work another one's undoing
Or even slight him at all anywhere:
And never let them wish each other ill
Through provocation or resentful thought."

And just as might a mother with her life
Protect the son that was her only child,
So let him then for every living thing
Maintain unbounded consciousness in being;
And let him too with love for all the world
Maintain unbounded consciousness in being
Above, below, and all round in between,
Untroubled, with no enemy or foe.
And while he stands or walks or while he sits
Or while he lies down, free from drowsiness,
Let him resolve upon this mindfulness:
This is Divine Abiding here, they say.

But when he has no trafficking with views,
Is virtuous, and has perfected seeing,
And purges greed for sensual desires,
He surely comes no more to any womb.

11. *Methodical Practice: from the Paṭisambhidāmagga (traditionally ascribed to the Arahat Sāriputta)*

The heart-deliverance of loving-kindness is practised with unspecified extension, with specified extension, and with directional extension.

That with unspecified extension is practised in five ways as follows: May all beings be freed from enmity, distress, and anxiety, and may they guide themselves to bliss.

May all breathing things ... all creatures ... all persons ... May all those who are embodied be freed from enmity, distress, and anxiety, and may they guide themselves to bliss.

That with specified extension is practised in seven ways as follows: May all women be freed from enmity, distress, and anxiety, and may they guide themselves to bliss. May all men ... all noble ones ... all who are not noble ones ... all deities ... all human beings ... May all those in the states of deprivation be freed from enmity, distress, and anxiety, and may they guide themselves to bliss.

That with directional extension is practised in ten ways as follows:

May all beings in the eastern direction be freed from enmity, distress, and anxiety, and may they guide themselves to bliss. May all beings in the western direction ... in the northern direction ... in the southern direction ... in the eastern intermediate direction ... in the western intermediate direction ... in the northern intermediate direction ... in the southern intermediate direction ... in the downward direction ... May all those in the upward direction be freed from enmity, distress, and anxiety, and may they guide themselves to bliss.

May all breathing things ... May all creatures ... May all persons ... May all who are embodied ... May all women

... May all men ... May all noble ones ... May all who are not noble ones ... May all deities ... May all human beings ...

May all those in the states of deprivation in the eastern direction be freed from enmity, distress, and anxiety, and may they guide themselves to bliss ... May all those in states of deprivation in the upward direction be freed from enmity, distress, and anxiety, and may they guide themselves to bliss.

12. *From the Abhidhamma Piṭaka, Appamaññavibhaṅga (traditionally ascribed to the Buddha)*

And how does a bhikkhu abide with his heart imbued with loving-kindness extending over one direction? Just as he would feel friendliness on seeing a dearly beloved person, so he extends loving-kindness to all creatures.

As Practised without Insight into the Four Noble Truths

13. *From the Majjhima Nikāya, Sutta 99 (spoken by the Buddha)*

"Master Gotama, I have heard it said that the Monk Gotama teaches the path to the retinue of the High Divinity. It would be good if Master Gotama would teach me that."

"Then listen and attend carefully to what I shall say."

"Even so, sir," the student Subha Todeyyaputta replied. The Blessed One said this:

"And what is the path to the retinue of the High Divinity? Here a bhikkhu abides with his heart imbued with loving-kindness extending over one quarter, likewise the second quarter, likewise the third quarter, likewise the fourth quarter, and so above, below, around, and everywhere and to all as to himself; he abides with his heart abundant, exalted, measureless in loving-kindness, without hostility or ill-will, extending over the all-encompassing world. While this heart-deliverance of loving-kindness is maintained in being in this way, no action restricted by limited measurement is found there, none persists there. Just as a vigorous trumpeter could easily make himself heard in the four directions, so too when the heart-deliverance of loving-kindness is maintained in being in this way no action restricted by limited measurement is found there, none persists there. This is the path to the retinue of the High Divinity."

As Practised with Insight into the Four Noble Truths

14. *From the Aṅguttara Nikāya, 4:125*
    (spoken by the Buddha)

Here, bhikkhus, a certain person abides with his heart imbued with loving-kindness extending over one quarter, likewise the second quarter, likewise the third quarter, likewise the fourth quarter, and so above, below, around, and everywhere, and to all as to himself; he abides with his heart abundant, exalted, measureless in loving-kindness, without hostility or ill-will, extending over the all-encompassing world.

He finds gratification in that, finds it desirable and looks to it for his well-being; steady and resolute thereon, he abides much in it, and if he dies without losing it, he reappears among the gods of a High Divinity's retinue.

Now the gods of a High Divinity's retinue have a lifespan of one aeon. An ordinary person (who has not attained the Noble Eightfold Path) stays there for his lifespan; but after he has used up the whole lifespan enjoyed by those gods, he leaves it all, and (according to what his past deeds may have been) he may go down even to hell, or to an animal womb, or to the ghost realm. But a disciple of the Perfect One stays there (in that heaven) for his lifespan, and after he has used up the whole lifespan enjoyed by those gods, he eventually attains complete extinction of lust, hate, and delusion in that same kind of heavenly existence.

It is this that distinguishes, that differentiates, the wise disciple who is ennobled (by attainment of the noble path) from the unwise ordinary man, when, that is to say, there is a destination for reappearance (after death, but an Arahat has made an end of birth).

15. *From the Aṅguttara Nikāya, 4:126*
    (spoken by the Buddha)

Here, bhikkhus, a certain person abides with his heart imbued with loving-kindness extending ... over the all-encompassing world.

Now whatever therein (during that state of contemplation) exists classifiable as form, classifiable as a feeling (of pleasure, pain, or neutrality), classifiable as perception, classifiable as determinative acts, or classifiable as consciousness, such things he sees as impermanent, as liable to suffering, as a disease, as a cancer, as a barb, as a calamity, as an affliction, as alien, as being worn away, as void, as not-self. On the dissolution of the body, after death, he reappears (as a non-returner) in the retinue of the Gods of the Pure Abodes (where there are only those who have reached the noble path and where extinction of greed, hate, and delusion is reached in less than seven lives without return to this world). And this kind of reappearance is not shared by ordinary men (who have not reached the Noble Eightfold Path).

The Arahat

16. *From the Aṅguttara Nikāya, 3:66*
    (spoken by the Arahat Nandaka)

Thus I heard. On one occasion the Venerable Nandaka was living at Sāvatthī in the Eastern Monastery, Migāra's Mother's Palace. Then Migāra's grandson, Sāÿha, and Pekhuniya's grandson, Rohana, went to the Venerable Nandaka, and after salutation they sat down at one side. When they had done so the Venerable Nandaka said to Migāra's grandson Sāÿha:

"Come, Sāÿha, do not be satisfied with hearsay or with tradition or with legendary lore or with what has come down in scriptures or with conjecture or with logical inference or with weighing evidence or with a liking for a view after pondering it or with someone else's ability or with the thought, 'The monk is our teacher.' When you know in yourself, 'These things are unprofitable, liable to censure, condemned by the wise, being adopted and put into effect, they lead to harm and suffering,' then you should abandon them. What do you think? Is there greed?"—"Yes, venerable sir."—"Covetousness is the meaning of that, I say. Through greed a covetous man kills breathing things, takes what is not given, commits adultery, and utters falsehood, and he gets another to do likewise. Will that be long for his harm and suffering?"— "Yes, venerable sir."—"What do you think, is there hate?"— "Yes, venerable sir."—"Ill-will is the meaning of that, I say. Through hate a malevolent man kills breathing things ... Will that be long for his harm and suffering?"—"Yes, venerable sir."—"What do you think? Is there delusion?" —"Yes, venerable sir."—"Ignorance is the meaning of that, I say. Through ignorance a deluded man kills breathing

things ... Will that be long for his harm and suffering?"—
"Yes, venerable sir."

"What do you think? Are these things profitable
or unprofitable?"—"Unprofitable, venerable sir."—
"Reprehensible or blameless?"—"Reprehensible,
venerable sir."—"Condemned or commended by the
wise?"— "Condemned by the wise, venerable sir."—"Being
adopted and put into effect, do they lead to harm and
suffering, or do they not, or how does it appear to you in
this case?"—"Being adopted and put into effect, venerable
sir, they lead to harm and suffering. So it appears in this
case."—"Now that was the reason why I told you 'Come,
Sāÿha, do not be satisfied with hearsay ... When you
know in yourself, 'These things are unprofitable,' then
you should abandon them."

"Come, Sāÿha, do not be satisfied with hearsay ...
or with the thought, 'The monk is our teacher.' When
you know in yourself, 'These things are profitable,
blameless, commended by the wise, being adopted and
put into effect they lead to welfare and happiness,' then
you should practise them and abide in them. What do
you think? Is there non-greed?"—"Yes, venerable sir."—
"Uncovetousness is the meaning of that, I say. Through
non-greed an uncovetous man does not kill breathing
things or take what is not given or commit adultery
or utter falsehood, and he gets another to do likewise.
Will that be long for his welfare and happiness?"—"Yes,
venerable sir."—"What do you think? Is there non-hate?"—
"Yes, venerable sir."—"Non ill-will is the meaning of that,
I say. Through non ill-will an unmalevolent man does not
kill breathing things ... Will that be long for his welfare
and happiness?"—"Yes, venerable sir."—"What do you
think? Is there non-delusion?"—"Yes, venerable sir."—
"True knowledge is the meaning of that, I say. Through

non-delusion a man with true knowledge does not kill breathing things ... Will that be long for his welfare and happiness?"—"Yes, venerable sir."

"What do you think? Are these things profitable or unprofitable?"—"Profitable, venerable sir."—"Reprehensible or blameless?"—"Blameless, venerable sir." —"Condemned or commended by the wise?"— "Commended by the wise, venerable sir."— "Being adopted and put into effect, do they lead to welfare and happiness, or do they not, or how does it appear to you in this case?"—"Being adopted and put into effect, venerable sir, they lead to welfare and happiness. So it appears to us in this case."—"Now that was the reason why I told you, 'Come Sāyha, do not be satisfied with hearsay ... when you know in yourself, 'These things are profitable ...' then you should practise them and abide in them."

"Now a disciple who is ennobled (by reaching the noble path), who has rid himself in this way of covetousness and ill-will and is undeluded, abides with his heart imbued with loving-kindness extending over one quarter, likewise the second quarter, likewise the third quarter, likewise the fourth quarter, and so above, below, around, and everywhere, and to all as to himself; he abides with his heart abundant, exalted, measureless in loving-kindness, without hostility or ill-will, extending over the all-encompassing world. He abides with his heart imbued with compassion ... gladness ... equanimity ... extending over the all-encompassing world. Now he understands this state of contemplation in this way: 'There is this (state of divine abiding in me who have entered the stream). There is what has been abandoned (which is the amount of greed, hate, and delusion exhausted by the stream-entry path). There is a superior goal (which is Arahatship). And there is an ultimate escape from this whole field of perception.'

"When he knows and sees in this way, his heart is liberated from the taint of sensual desire, from the taint of being, and from the taint of ignorance. When liberated (by reaching the Arahat path), there comes thereafter the knowledge that it is liberated. He knows that birth is ended, that the divine life has been lived out, that what had to be done is done, and that there is no more of this to come. He understands thus: 'Formerly there was greed which was bad, and now there is none, which is good. Formerly there was hate, which was bad, and now there is none, which is good. Formerly there was delusion, which was bad, and now there is none, which is good.' So here and now in this very life he is parched no more (by the fever of craving's thirst, his fires of greed, hate and delusion are) extinguished and cooled out; experiencing bliss, he abides (for the remainder of his last lifespan) divinely pure in himself."

ABOUT PARIYATTI

Pariyatti is dedicated to providing affordable access to authentic teachings of the Buddha about the Dhamma theory (*pariyatti*) and practice (*paṭipatti*) of Vipassana meditation. A 501(c)(3) nonprofit charitable organization since 2002, Pariyatti is sustained by contributions from individuals who appreciate and want to share the incalculable value of the Dhamma teachings. We invite you to visit www.pariyatti.org to learn about our programs, services, and ways to support publishing and other undertakings.

Pariyatti Publishing Imprints

Vipassana Research Publications (focus on Vipassana as taught by S.N. Goenka in the tradition of Sayagyi U Ba Khin)

BPS Pariyatti Editions (selected titles from the Buddhist Publication Society, copublished by Pariyatti in the Americas)

Pariyatti Digital Editions (audio and video titles, including discourses)

Pariyatti Press (classic titles returned to print and inspirational writing by contemporary authors)

Pariyatti enriches the world by

- disseminating the words of the Buddha,
- providing sustenance for the seeker's journey,
- illuminating the meditator's path.

Printed in Great Britain
by Amazon